The EVERYTHING KIDS'
Fun with Food
Placemats
SUPER SPORTS

Puzzles, games, jokes, and more for tons of mealtime fun!

home— or on the go!

Aadamsmedia
Avon, Massachusetts

An Everything® Series product.
Everything® and everything.com® are registered
trademarks of F+W Media, Inc.

Published by Adams Media,
a division of F+W Media, Inc.
57 Littlefield Street
Avon, MA 02322. U.S.A.
www.adamsmedia.com

Contains material adapted and abridged from *The Every-
thing® KIDS' Baseball Book, 6th Edition* by Greg Jacobs,
copyright © 2010 by F+W Media, Inc., ISBN 13: 978-1-
60550-641-8, ISBN 10: 1-60550-641-9; *The Everything® Kid's
Basketball Book* by Bob Schaller with Coach Dave Harnish,
copyright © 2009 by F+W Media, Inc., ISBN 13: 978-1-
60550-165-9, ISBN 10: 1-60550-165-4; *The Everything® KIDS'
Connect the Dots Puzzle and Activity Book* by Scot Ritchie,
copyright © 2008 by F+W Media, Inc., ISBN 13: 978-1-
59869-647-9, ISBN 10: 1-59869-647-5; *The Everything® KIDS'
Crazy Puzzles Book* by Beth L. Blair and Jennifer A. Ericsson, copyright © 2005 by F+W Media, Inc., ISBN 13: 978-1-
59337-631-0, ISBN 10: 1-59337-361-9; *The Everything® KIDS'
Football Book, 2nd Edition* by Greg Jacobs, copyright © 2010
by F+W Media, Inc., ISBN 13: 978-1-4405-0413-6, ISBN 10:
1-4405-0413-X; *The Everything® KIDS' More Amazing Mazes
Book* by Beth L. Blair and Jennifer A. Ericsson, copyright
© 2010 by F+W Media, Inc., ISBN 13: 978-1-4405-0150-0,
ISBN 10: 1-4405-0150-5; *The Everything® KIDS' More Puzzles Book* by Scot Ritchie, copyright © 2010 by F+W Media,
Inc., ISBN 13: 978-1-4405-0647-5, ISBN 10: 1-4405-0647-
7; *The Everything® KIDS' Riddles and Brain Teasers Book* by
Kathi Wagner and Aubrey Wagner, copyright © 2004
by F+W Media, Inc., ISBN 13: 978-1-59337-036-7, ISBN 10:
1-59337-036-9; *The Everything® KIDS' Soccer Book, 2nd Edition* by Deborah W. Crisfield, copyright © 2009 by F+W
Media, Inc., ISBN 13: 978-1-60550-162-8, ISBN 10: 1-60550-
162-X; *The Everything® KIDS' Word Search Puzzle and Activity Book* by Beth L. Blair and Jennifer Ericsson, copyright
© 2008 by F+W Media, Inc., ISBN 13: 978-1-59869-545-8,
ISBN 10: 1-59869-545-2.

ISBN 10: 1-4405-2884-5
ISBN 13: 978-1-4405-2884-2

Printed by RR Donnelley, Shenzhen, China.

10 9 8 7 6 5 4 3 2 1

June 2011

This product is available at quantity discounts
for bulk purchases.
For information, please call 1-800-289-0963.

PLAY BALL!

Name Game

This baseball card collector has gotten some pretty famous autographs. Unfortunately, the players signed their names too big! Can you tell who signed each card? Choose names from the list.

Barry Bonds
Willie Mays
Nolan Ryan
Pete Rose
Alex Rodriguez
Cy Young
Sandy Koufax
Ty Cobb
Jimmie Foxx
Tom Seaver
Greg Maddux
Lou Gehrig
Hank Aaron

The Original 1876 National League

1876 Team Name	Modern Team Name
Chicago White Stockings	Chicago Cubs
Philadelphia Athletics	The Philadelphia Athletics only played in the NL in 1876.
Boston Red Stockings	Atlanta Braves
Hartford Dark Blues	The Hartford Dark Blues only played in the NL in 1876 and 1877.
Mutual of New York	Mutual of New York only played in the NL in 1876.
St. Louis Brown Stockings	The St. Louis Brown Stockings only played in the NL in 1876 and 1877.
Cincinnati Red Stockings	The Cincinnati Red Stockings only played in the NL from 1876–1880.
Louisville Grays	The Louisville Grays only played in the NL in 1876 and 1877.

Curve Ball

The curve ball is one of the trickiest pitches to hit. See if you can score by running a line of color through each of the curvy baseball terms in the following list! Instead of reading in a straight line, each word has <u>one</u> bend in it. Words can go in any direction.

HINT: One word has been done for you.

ASTROTURF
~~BLEACHERS~~
DUGOUT
HOME RUN
HOTDOG
POP FLY
SCOREBOARD
SHORTSTOP
STADIUM
WORLD SERIES

```
F L Y L E B O A R D T O
U P O R R L E R N P O P
G R O M F E S E I R E S
A C U P D A T S C T M D
S S T G I C O S H I R L
T K R U U H H N D S N R
R B O E M O R E P U T O
I O U S R H O T R S G W
H O T T S T O P E S O O
O M D U U H O T M T U B
T D O L R K M M O A T L
R O G D B F E O H D M A
```

Game Pieces

Baseball is such a familiar game that you might not even need words to describe it! Study the four picture puzzles below and see if you can figure out what baseball term, player, or place they each describe.

ANSWERS

Name Game

Nolan Ryan — ol ya

Greg Maddux — eg ux

Willie Mays — il ay

Ty Cobb — Ty ob

Jimmie Foxx — mi ox

Alex Rodriguez — ex ri

Curve Ball

```
F L Y L E B O A R D T O
U P O R R L E R N P O P
G R O M F E S E I R E S
A C U P D A T S C T M D
S S T G I C O S H I R L
T K R U U H H N D S N R
R B O E M O R E P U T O
I O U S R H O T R S G W
H O T T S T O P E S O O
O M D U U H O T M T U B
T D O L R K M M O A T L
R O G D B F E O H D M A
```

Game Pieces

fly ball

southpaw

home run

bullpen

BRAIN BLITZ

Perfect Play

Give yourself six points if you can match this touchdown to its perfect shadow!

WORDS to KNOW

THE MERGER: Officially, the AFL merged with the NFL in 1970, even though they had played championship games since the 1966 season. You will often hear broadcasters refer to events "since the merger." Though team and individual statistics before 1970 are official and do count in the record books, the year of the merger represents when the NFL started to resemble the league you watch today.

WILD CARD: Before 1970, the only teams in the playoffs were the division winners. In the 1970 season, the two teams in each conference with the best records that were not division winners were invited to the playoffs. These teams played each other in the wild card game. The winner of that game advanced to play a division winner.

Brush Up

This coach is giving one of his players a compliment—or is he? To find out what the coach is saying, you must write all the letters from the scattered pieces into their proper spaces in the grid. Hint: Try matching the pattern of the black boxes!

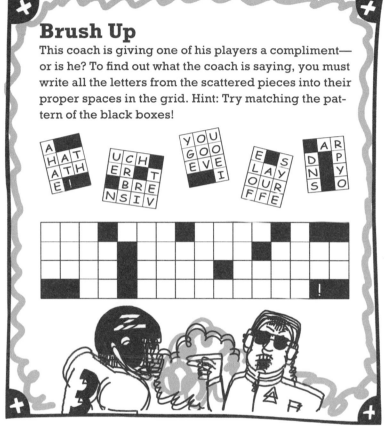

Fractured Football

The linebacker hit this football so hard it was broken in half! Which two pieces will fit together to make one complete ball?

Football GREAT

The Undefeated 1972 Dolphins

In 1972, the Miami Dolphins became the first team to win every game in a season. The team capped its 14-0 regular season with three postseason victories, including a 14-7 victory over the Redskins in Super Bowl VII. Members of the 1972 Dolphins still celebrate together each season after the last undefeated team loses a game.

ANSWERS

Perfect Play

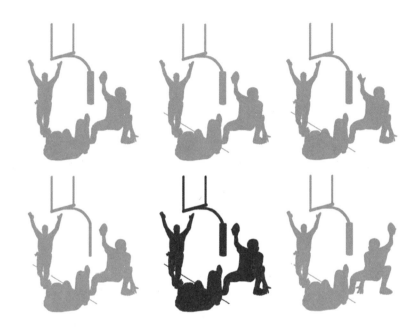

Brush Up

YOU ARE SUCH A GOOD PLAYER THAT EVEN YOUR BREATH IS OFFENSIVE!

Fractured Football

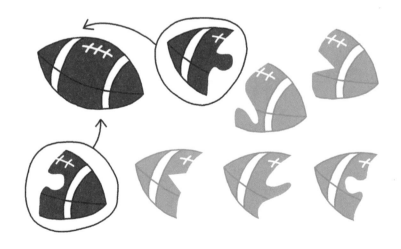

BULLPEN BRAIN TEASERS

Done to a T-Ball

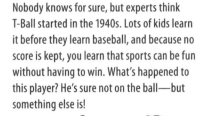

Nobody knows for sure, but experts think T-Ball started in the 1940s. Lots of kids learn it before they learn baseball, and because no score is kept, you learn that sports can be fun without having to win. What's happened to this player? He's sure not on the ball—but something else is!

What animal is the best at hitting baseballs? A bat!

Baseball Biggies

Somebody has messed up these big baseball names. Can you find the correct first letter to finish their last names?

All-Time Record Holders

These records are correct as of the start of the 2010 season.

Hitting

All-Time Batting Average Leaders

1. Ty Cobb .366
2. Rogers Hornsby .358
3. "Shoeless" Joe Jackson .356
4. Lefty O'Doul .349
5. Ed Delahanty .346
6. Tris Speaker .345
7. Ted Williams .344
8. Billy Hamilton .344
9. Dan Brouthers .342
10. Babe Ruth .342

A player must have more than 3,000 plate appearances to qualify for this list.

All-Time RBI Leaders

1. Hank Aaron 2,297
2. Babe Ruth 2,213
3. Cap Anson 2,076
4. Barry Bonds 1,996
5. Lou Gehrig 1,995
6. Stan Musial 1,951
7. Ty Cobb 1,938
8. Jimmie Foxx 1,922
9. Eddie Murray 1,917
10. Willie Mays 1,903

It's All in the Name

This baseball team has decided to call itself the Kangaroos. Sherry suggested a 9-letter name because there are 9 players on the team. Another player thought the name should also have at least 1 letter from each player's name. Can you tell who's on the team?

KYRA MICHELLE PHIL GRAHAM

KANGAROOS

ALYSSA DANIEL EMMY JORGE
ABDUL JULIE TIM
LILY
GLORIA ROBERT
SHERRY

FUN FACT

The Minor Leagues

Each major league team supports several minor league teams, which played even through the strike of 1994. Almost every player spends a few years in the minors before coming to the major leagues. Some players are sent back down to the minor leagues if they are not playing well, and sometimes good major league players will go to the minors after an injury to get used to playing again. Minor league teams are in many smaller cities across the country.

ANSWERS

Done to a T-Ball

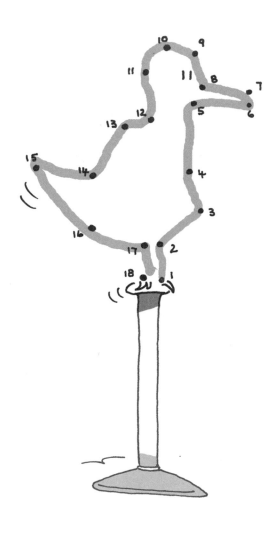

It's All in the Name

Kyra, Alyssa, Daniel, Jorge, Abdul, Graham, Robert, Gloria, and Sherry are all on the team.

Baseball Biggies

Ruth, Mays, Paige, Cobb, Young, Mantle, Aaron, Gehrig, DiMaggio, Musial

WORDS to KNOW

TAILGATING: A tailgate party is a picnic in the stadium parking lot before a game. This can be as simple as eating some sandwiches out of a cooler while sitting on the back of your car. Elaborate tailgaters bring lawn chairs, big grills, and four-course meals. Part of the fun is being with all the other tailgating fans of your team. Bring extra food to share, and you'll meet some interesting folks!

What's in a Name?

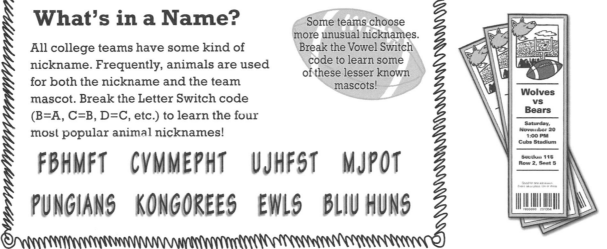

All college teams have some kind of nickname. Frequently, animals are used for both the nickname and the team mascot. Break the Letter Switch code (B=A, C=B, D=C, etc.) to learn the four most popular animal nicknames!

FBHMFT   CVMMEPHT   UJHFST   MJPOT

PUNGIANS   KONGOREES   EWLS   BLIU HUNS

Some teams choose more unusual nicknames. Break the Vowel Switch code to learn some of these lesser known mascots!

Wolves vs Bears

Saturday, November 20
1:00 PM
Cubs Stadium

Section 116
Row 2, Seat 5

FUN FACT

Monday Night Football
In the 1960s and 1970s, no more than two games were shown on TV each Sunday. In 1970, ABC started showing one game every Monday night, using their best announcers and lots of cameras and graphics to produce a big show. Monday Night Football lasted until 2005 on ABC, and every week it was one of the top ten most-watched TV shows. Now, MNF is on ESPN with the top-rated announcing team of Mike Tirico, John Gruden, and Ron Jaworski.

The Heidi Game
At 7:00 P.M. on November 17, 1968, the Jets took a five-point lead on the Raiders with sixty-five seconds to go. Though a football game usually takes only about three hours to play, this one was taking longer. NBC television had planned to air the movie *Heidi* at 7:00, so they stopped showing the football game and showed the movie. Fans, especially in New York, were furious. So many people called NBC to complain that NBC issued an apology and changed their rules to show entire football games, no matter the length of the game.

Go Team!

A very visible part of any football team are the cheerleaders! The first organized cheer was during a college football game over 100 years ago, in 1898. Believe it or not, that original cheer is still being used at the University of Minnesota today! Use the decoder to fill in the blanks, and then give this cheer a try— outside the house, of course!

A = ☀
H = ★
I = ☆
N = ☆
O = ✳
S = ✳
Y = ◉

R✳★, R✳★, R✳★!
✳K☆-U-M✳★,
★★★-R✳★!
★★★-R✳★!
V✳R✳☆T◉!
V✳R✳☆T◉!
V✳R✳☆T◉,
M☆★✳-E-✳★-T✳★!

Super Sized

Use the picture and letter equations to spell out the silly answer to this riddle.

What kind of football player wears the biggest helmet?

THE 1 [witch] -C

THE B+ [pig] -P +GEST

H+ [bread] -BR !

EVERYTHING KIDS'

ANSWERS

What's in a Name?

The most popular mascots are:

EAGLES BULLDOGS TIGERS LIONS

Some more unusual mascots are:

PENGUINS KANGAROOS OWLS BLUE HENS

Super Sized

The one with the biggest head!

Go Team!

**RAH, RAH, RAH!
SKI-U-MAH,
HOO-RAH!
HOO-RAH!
VARSITY!
VARSITY!
VARSITY,
MINN-E-SO-TAH!**

"Ski-U-Mah" is pronounced "SKY-YOU-MAH." "Ski" is a Native American battle cry meaning "victory." "U-Mah" represents the <u>U</u>niversity of <u>M</u>innesota.

KICKIN' IT

Keep Your Eye on the Ball

All thirteen of the words in this puzzle can be followed by the word BALL. See how many words you can figure out and fit into the criss-cross grid.

HINT: We've left you the first letter of each!

Soccer   Wiffle   Basket

Base   Ping Pong   Snow

Foot   Tee   Bowling

Golf   Tether

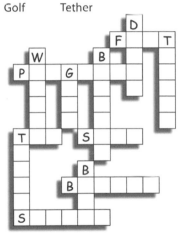

We're with You!

This team is really supporting their keeper! Using a simple number substitution code (A=1, B=2, etc.) figure out what the team is spelling out with the numbers on their jerseys.

A goalie shirt to draw on

JOKIN' AROUND

QUESTION: Why won't Cinderella ever be a great soccer goalkeeper?

ANSWER: She runs away from the ball.

Uniform Uniforms

Oops—goalies are supposed to wear shirts that are different from the rest of the team. These goalies look too much alike! Cross out the three pairs of goalies who are wearing exactly the same shirts. Circle the one goalie who has a shirt that is different from everyone else's. This goalie will get to play today!

FUN FACT

The Soccer-Style Kick

Many beginning players use their toes to kick the ball because it gives them more distance than the instep. This is a mistake. If you practice the instep pass, it won't take you long until it's just as powerful as the toe-poke, and it's certainly a whole lot more accurate, as a Hungarian football player named Pete Gogolak showed the NFL. Until he came along, field goal kickers were kicking with their toes. Coming from Hungary, Pete had played soccer, so his long kicks were all soccer-style. He was so successful that now, a soccer-style instep kick is all you see—in *both* soccer and football.

FUN FACT

The Seal Dribble

One very unusual method of dribbling is called the seal dribble. This entails moving the ball down the field by bouncing it off your head. Obviously this is a very advanced skill, but it's a real problem for defenders because they have a hard time interfering with the player in a legal way. They can't go after the ball because it's up at head level, and they can't go after the body, without being called for a foul.

ANSWERS

Keep Your Eye on the Ball

We're with You!

WAY TO GO, GOALIE!

Uniform Uniforms

Today's Goalie

Hard Ball

Baseball is a game full of action! Fill in as many wild words as you can, using the across and down clues. We left you some T-O-U-G-H letters and words as hints!

ACROSS

3. Fun baseball game played against an upright surface.
6. Team name: Pittsburgh
7. Nickname for a powerful hitter.
11. Smooth, round stick used to hit a baseball.
13. The 37-foot-high wall in Boston's Fenway Park.
16. A "_____ hitter" is a hitter who hits for someone else.
17. To run from one base to another before the next player at bat has hit the ball.
19. Team name: San Francisco _____.
21. If the hitter bunts with a man on third base, it's called a "_____ play."

DOWN

1. Joe DiMaggio's nickname: "_____'n Joe."
2. When a hitter stops getting hits for a while.
4. Hank Aaron's nickname: "The _____."
5. "The _____" is when fans stand and then sit while moving their arms up and down in a motion that goes all around the stadium.
6. A "_____" fly goes high up in the air and is easily caught.
7. Sharp bumps on the bottom of baseball players' shoes.
8. "The Seventh Inning _____" gives fan a chance to get up and move around.
9. Team name: Los Angeles _____.
10. The score made by a player who touches first, second, third, and home base.
11. Jose Conseco and Mark McGwire were known as the "_____ Brothers."
12. A ball hit out of fair territory.
14. A _____ play is when a player is trapped between two bases. He has to scramble to get to one base or the other before being tagged out.
15. A "_____ ball" is the speediest pitch.
18. A player will sometimes have to _____ headfirst into a base to avoid being tagged out.
20. A "grand _____" is a home run hit when bases are loaded.

Running Home

Baseball is another fast sport that's great fun to play. There's nothing like hitting the ball and racing around the bases to get a home run. Be careful on this puzzle—instead of numbers, you will be connecting letters. Make sure you connect the right A to the right B; there are lots to choose from.

The fastest recorded time circling the bases was set way back in 1932, by Evar Swanson. He hit the ball, ran from first to second to third and made it to home base in 13.3 seconds. It looks like somebody was there to record it, too!

Do you see a **pattern** here? Number of **catchers** on a baseball team, number of **teams** in a game, number of **strikes** before an out, number of **bases** in a diamond.

1, 2, 3, 4

Dugout

One letter has been dug out of each of the following common baseball words. Fill in the missing letters. Then, transfer those letters to the corresponding boxes in the grid to form the answer to this riddle:

What's another nickname for a baseball bat?

1. UNI_ORM
2. G_OVE
3. PLA_OFF
4. _LIDE
5. S_ING
6. F_N
7. BUN_
8. CA_CHER
9. ST_AL
10. _UN

1	2	3	4	5	6	7	8	9	10

The Original 1876 American League

1876 Team Name	Modern Team Name
Chicago White Stockings	Chicago White Sox
Boston Americans	Boston Red Sox
Detroit Tigers	Detroit Tigers
Philadelphia Athletics	Oakland Athletics
Baltimore Orioles	New York Yankees
Washington Senators	Minnesota Twins
Cleveland Blues	Cleveland Indians
Milwaukee Brewers	Baltimore Orioles

EVERYTHING KIDS

ANSWERS

Hard Ball

Running Home

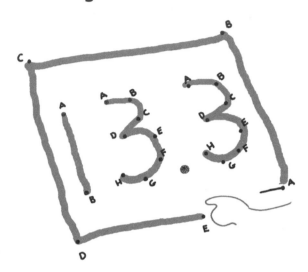

Dugout

1. UNI_F_ORM
2. G_L_OVE
3. PLA_Y_OFF
4. _S_LIDE
5. S_W_ING

6. F_A_N
7. BUN_T_
8. CA_T_CHER
9. ST_E_AL
10. _R_UN

¹F	²L	³Y	⁴S	⁵W	⁶A	⁷T	⁸T	⁹E	¹⁰R

RECEIVER RIDDLES

Twin Teammates

There are ten differences between the uniforms and equipment shown here. Can you find them?

DID YOU KNOW? Some players who carry the ball wear very tight pants. This makes it harder for the other team to grab their pants to stop them!

Where's the Player?

Break the Last to First code to read this silly riddle and its silly answer!

hatW si het
ifferenced
etweenb a
ootballf layerp
nda a uckd?

ou'llY indf neo
ni a uddleh,
nda het thero
ni a uddlep!

Football GREAT

Howie Long

Howie enjoyed a thirteen-year career as a dominating defensive lineman with the Oakland Raiders. He went to eight Pro Bowls and was honored by the NFL in its all-1980s team. After his football career, he became a well-known television studio host. Howie attended Milford High School in Massachusetts, where he participated in football, baseball, and track, and earned a membership in the Milford hall of fame. His son Chris is now a defensive lineman for the St. Louis Rams.

FUN FACT

The Stanford Axe
At a Cal-Stanford baseball game in 1899, Cal students stole an axe from the Stanford cheerleaders. Cal kept that axe in a bank vault for thirty-one years, until a crew of Stanford students launched an elaborate and successful plot to steal it back. Now, whichever team wins the Big Game gets to keep the axe for a year. At Stanford pep rallies, cheerleaders still refer to "the Stanford Axe that California has wrongly stolen from us, that it is our responsibility to retrieve."

Rivalry Story
Legendary Ohio State coach Woody Hayes hated Michigan—not just the university, but the whole state and anything associated with it. It is said that when the Ohio State team bus was running out of gas on the way home to Ohio, Coach Hayes refused to stop at any gas station in the state of Michigan, even if he might have to walk for miles to get more gas.

Words to Play By

Place all the letters into their proper spaces in the empty grid. You will see that this familiar saying is true both on and off the football field!

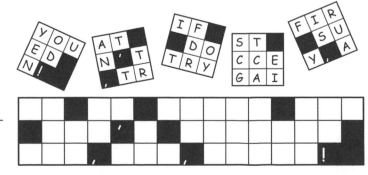

ANSWERS

Twin Teammates

Where's the Player?

What is the difference between a football player and a duck?

· · · · · · · · · · · · · · · · ·

You'll find one in a huddle, and the other in a puddle!

Words to Play By

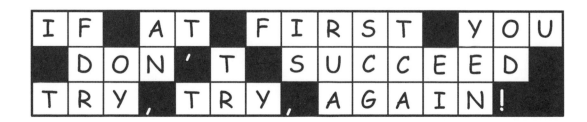

IF AT FIRST YOU DON'T SUCCEED TRY, TRY, AGAIN!

DRIBBLE DISTRACTIONS

Move the Ball

Dribble your way around the cones from **START** to **GOAL**. Avoid bumping into other members from your team who are practicing at the same time.

START

GOAL!

Opposite Offense

Here's a funny conversation between two soccer players. All the words that are underlined actually mean the opposite! Above each underlined word or group of words, write a word that means the opposite.

"Hey <u>here</u>, Lucas!"

"<u>Good-bye</u>, Caitlin!"

"How are <u>me</u>?"

"<u>You</u> <u>haven't</u> a <u>good</u> <u>hot</u>."

"How <u>wonderful</u>! I hope you <u>give</u> <u>worse</u> <u>a long time from now</u>."

"<u>You</u>, too. I <u>did</u> <u>wake</u> <u>none</u> <u>day</u> <u>short</u>."

"Oh, that's too <u>good</u>.

Well, <u>you</u> <u>haven't</u> to <u>come</u>. <u>Hello</u>!"

"<u>Hello</u>. See <u>me</u> <u>sooner</u>."

FUN FACT

The Argentine Indirect Kick

During the 1998 World Cup, Argentina used a tremendously successful indirect kick play. The other team had set up a wall. Argentina placed a man on the inside of the wall. A second player ran at the ball from the side, but stepped over it, not touching it. He then ran right across in front of the wall. Everyone's eyes were on this runner, but nobody was moving because the ball hadn't been touched yet. While everyone was watching this runner, the player next to the wall snuck around in back of it. That's when a third player stepped up and made a pass to him. He received it and popped in the goal. The first runner had been nothing but a decoy.

Speed Drill

This tiny picture puzzle shows where the goalie is allowed to use her hands. Where is that?

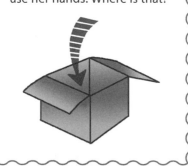

JOKIN' AROUND

FIRST SOCCER PLAYER:
Boy, these new cleats sure hurt.

SECOND SOCCER PLAYER:
That's because you're wearing them on the wrong feet.

FIRST SOCCER PLAYER:
I can't be. These are the only feet I have!

ANSWERS

Move the Ball

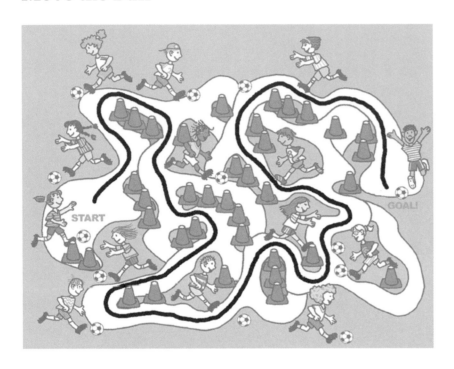

Opposite Offense

"Hey ~~here~~ *there*, Lucas!"

"~~Good-bye~~ *Hello*, Caitlin!"

"How are ~~me~~ *you*?"

"~~You haven't~~ *I have* a ~~good hot~~ *bad cold*."

"How ~~wonderful~~ *awful*! I

hope you ~~give worse~~ *get better*

~~a long time from now~~ *soon*."

"~~You~~ *Me*, too. I ~~did wake~~ *didn't sleep*

~~none day short~~ *all night long*."

"Oh, that's too ~~good~~ *bad*.

Well, ~~you haven't~~ *I have* to

~~come~~ *go*. ~~Hello~~ *Good-bye*!"

"~~Hello~~ *Good-bye*. See ~~me sooner~~ *you later*."

Speed Drill

Answer: in the box

FUNKY FREE KICKS

Speed Drill

How should a pass receiver be? This tiny picture puzzle shows how!

WELCOME

Fast Pass

Use your instep to start the ball driving down the field to a teammate. Continue alternating foot to ball until the path reaches the goal at the other end of the field. You can move up and down, or side to side, but not diagonally. If you hit a player's hand, a foul is called and you have to start again!

Extra skill play: Using just your finger to trace the path, see how long it takes you to do this puzzle. Try again in 10 minutes and see if it takes you just as long. Try again ten minutes after that. What's your best time?

START

GOAL!

JOKIN' AROUND

A not-so-smart fan arrives at a soccer game partway through the second half.

"What's the score?" he asks his friend as he settles into his seat.

"Zero to zero," comes the reply.

"And what was the score at halftime?" he asks.

FUN FACT

Just a Kid

At the age of 14, Freddy Adu became the youngest person to ever play for a professional sports team in the United States. He was signed by the DC United. Not surprisingly, he also became the youngest person to ever score a goal for MLS, which he also did at age 14.

I Spy Soccer

Be on the lookout for the word SOCCER hiding in this grid! There is only one time where all six letters appear in a row. Look forward, backward, up, down, and diagonally. It could be anywhere!

```
S R O S O S O C C E
O O R O S O C C E S
C E C C O C C O R O
C S O C E C E S O C
R O S E R E R O S S
S S O C C O S E O O
O C C S O C E C C C
C E R O C O C C C E
C O O C S E O O S E
E C O S R O C C O S
```

EVERYTHING KIDS

ANSWERS

Speed Drill

Answer: open and welcoming

Fast Pass

START

GOAL!

I Spy Soccer

```
S R O S O S O C C E
O O R O S O C C E S
C E C C O C C O R O
C S O C E C E S O C
R O S E R E R O S S
S S O C C O S E O O
O C C S O C E C C C
C E R O C O C C E E
C O O C S E O O S E
E C O S R O C C O S
```

PLAYOFF PUZZLES

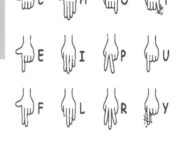

How come Drew never finishes a baseball game?

To find out, cross out all the words that have three letters or the letter U!

AND	EVERY	CAT
TIME	GOT	HE
BAT	GETS	FAR
TO	FUR	THIRD
BUT	BASE	HIT
HE	HAT	GOES
HUT	HOME	BAG

Lucky Numbers

Baseball is a game full of numbers. There's the RBI and ERA numbers, the numbers on the scoreboard, and of course the lucky number on the shirt of your favorite player!

In this tricky little puzzle, you must figure out what lucky combination of numbers to use so that each column (up and down) or row (across) adds up to the right totals shown in the white numbers. The white arrows show you in which direction you will be adding. Lucky you—four numbers are in place to get you started!

Here are the rules:

- You are only adding the numbers in any set of white boxes that are touching each other.
- Use only the numbers 1 through 9. Each number can only be used once in each set.
- Remember that each answer has to be correct both across *and* down!

Secret Signals

Use the decoder to figure out what message the catcher signaled to the pitcher when the crab came up to bat.

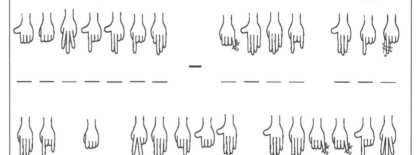

Name Change

In 1919, the Chicago White Sox were accused of being paid to lose the World Series! After that, the team became known by another name. Fill in all the letters that are not W-H-I-T-E to find out what it was.

BWLHAICTKESOX

Perfect Game

A pitcher pitches a perfect game when he gets every batter out for a whole game. That's only happened 17 times in the major leagues— and only once in the World Series.

FUN FACT

Best of Seven

The World Series is played as a best-of-seven series: This means that the first team to win four games wins the series, and there can't be more than seven games. In 1903, and again in 1918 through 1920, the series was played as best of nine, but it was changed back to today's best-of-seven format.

EVERYTHING KIDS®

ANSWERS

How come Drew . . .

~~AND~~	EVERY	~~CAT~~
TIME	~~GOT~~	HE
~~BAT~~	GETS	~~EAR~~
TO	~~FUR~~	THIRD
~~BUT~~	BASE	~~HIT~~
HE	~~HAT~~	GOES
~~HUT~~	HOME	~~BAG~~

Lucky Numbers

9↓	24↓		27↓	13↓
5→ 4	1	12→	5	7
11→ 5	6	15→ 6↓	9	6
17→	3	6	8	
15↓ 16→ 7	9	12→	4	8 11↓
13→ 8	5	4→	1	3

Name Change

BWLHAICTKESOX

Secret Signals

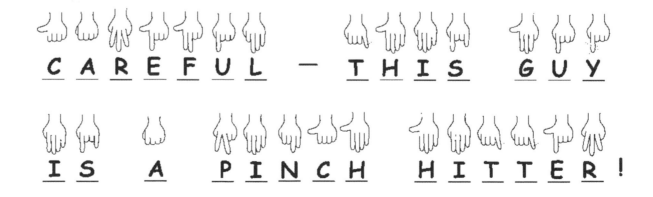

C A R E F U L — T H I S   G U Y

I S   A   P I N C H   H I T T E R !

EXTRA-POINT ACTIVITIES

Run Like Crazy

Get the running back to the end zone before he is tackled

GOAL

Most Valuable Player

What kind of football career will this player have? To figure out what the coach tells him, fill in the blanks with the numbered words.

Hey, Coach!

I want to

play 1_____,

2_____,

and 3_____!

OK — 4_____ at the

1_____ of

the 7_____ ,

2_____ the

6_____ 8_____ ,

and 3_____

9_____ who gets

5_____ it!

5 NEAR

3 TACKLE

6 WATER

7 BENCH

1 END

8 BUCKET

2 GUARD

4 SIT

9 ANYONE

Fans Have Fun

Football fans really get into cheering on their team! Can you find your way from START to END through the crazy crowd?

START

END

Football GREAT

Joe Montana

Joe Cool, as he became known, started his career with the San Francisco 49ers in 1979. In only his third year, he led the 49ers to their best NFL season ever: a 13-3 record and a playoff berth. Joe was named the most valuable player in three of his four Super Bowl victories. Throughout his career, Joe was known for his grace under pressure. Twenty-six times he led the 49ers to come-from-behind wins. That's where the nickname Joe Cool came from. Even when his team trailed, they believed Joe could lead them back.

WORDS to KNOW

POCKET: When the quarterback has dropped back to pass, his offensive line forms a horseshoe-shaped pocket around him. They push the pass rushers toward the sidelines and down the field, keeping the area around the quarterback clear of defenders until the quarterback can throw a pass.

ANSWERS

Run Like Crazy

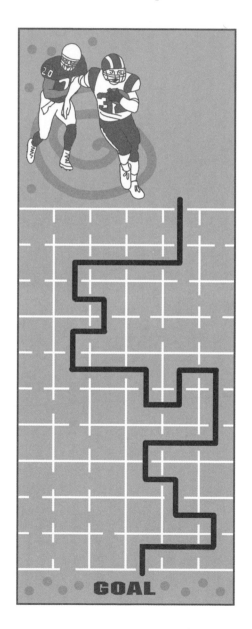

Most Valuable Player

"Hey, Coach! I want to play <u>END</u>, <u>GUARD</u>, and <u>TACKLE</u>."

"OK — <u>SIT</u> at the <u>END</u> of the <u>BENCH</u>, <u>GUARD</u> the <u>WATER</u> <u>BUCKET</u>, and <u>TACKLE</u> <u>ANYONE</u> who gets <u>NEAR</u> it!"

Fans Have Fun

PENALTY KICK PUZZLES

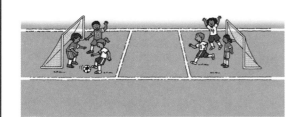

Teamwork

It takes two players to make a successful pass. And it takes two halves to make a successful compound word! Listed below are two sets of three-letter words. First unscramble the words in column A. Then, match each word in column A with a word in column B to form a new word. We've done the first one for you.

HINT: *The word in column A should always come first.*

A	B	
~~YEE~~	BID	EYELID
ORF	ROT	
NPA	AGE	
ONT	FIT	
RAC	TRY	
OTC	~~LID~~	
AMN	ICE	
UTO	TON	

JOKIN' AROUND

Two friends get to the stadium just before a big game between the New York MetroStars and D.C. United. The first friend says, "I wish I'd brought our piano to the stadium."

"Why would you bring a piano to a soccer game?" asks the second friend.

"Because I left the tickets on it."

Speed Drill

This tiny picture puzzle shows the important first step of any pass. What is it?

Practice, Practice, Practice

First, read this advice from Michelle Akers, a U.S. Women's World Cup player. She says, "My suggestion is to use your [weaker foot] as much as possible. That means use it all the time, every time, for everything you do on the soccer field. Use it in warm-up, for dribbling, shooting, receiving, in drills, when you train extra, etc. Whatever you are doing, use only your [weak] foot."

Now, figure out where to put each of the scrambled letters in the following puzzle. They all fit in spaces under their own column. When you have filled in the grid, you will be able to see what Michelle Akers promises this practicing will help you do!

B	F			T		O		T	I			O	C	E		P	U		3
I	E	S		N	D	A	F	G	H	T	S	U	U	R	Y	U	O	A	I	y
D	H	E	Y	U	O	O	O	H	T	E	O	C	N	A	O	O	E	E	B	B	L
T	A	A	A	S	W	F	I	T	H	S	I	G	R	A	W	L	E	Y	E	R	O

FUN FACT

Player of the Year . . . Again

It's not hard to argue the point that Landon Donovan is the best men's soccer player ever to come from the United States. He won the Honda Player of the year award four times (2002, 2003, 2004, and 2007), and became the youngest person ever to achieve 50 goals and 50 assists. He is also the all-time leading scorer for the U.S. National Team with 35 goals. Currently he plays for the Los Angeles Galaxy.

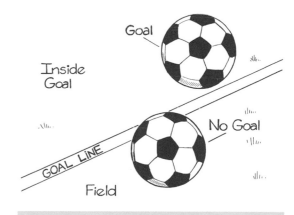

Goal

Inside Goal

No Goal

GOAL LINE

Field

Official goal

ANSWERS

Teamwork

A	B
~~YEE~~	BID
ORF	ROT
NPA	AGE
ONT	FIT
RAC	TRY
OTC	~~LID~~
AMN	ICE
UTO	TON

EYELID
FORBID
PANTRY
NOTICE
CARROT
COTTON
MANAGE
OUTFIT

Practice, Practice, Practice

B	F			T		O		T	I	T			O		C		E			P					3	
I	E		S	N	D	O	A	F	G	H	H	T	E	D	S	O	G	C	R	U	Y		O	O	A	E	I	Y
D	H	E	Y	U	T	D	O	F	O	O	H	T	E	D	S	F	G	C	U	A	R	T	H	R	W	H	O	L	E
T	A	Y	A	E	S	W	R	F	I	T	T	H	H	S	I	M	O	R	A	T	H	R	W	E	B	E	L	R	L

I	F		Y	O	U		D	O		T	H	I	S		F	O	R		A		W	H	O	L	E		3	0	
D	A	Y	S		S	T	R	A	I	G	H	T	,		I		G	U	A	R	A	N	T	E	E		B	Y	
T	H	E		E	N	D		O	F		T	H	E		M	O	N	T	H		Y	O	U		W	I	L	L	
B	E		A		T	W	O	-	F	O	O	T	E	D		S	O	C	C	E	R		P	L	A	Y	E	R	.

Speed Drill

Answer: a plant

BATTER UP!

Switch Hitter

Can you see the 10 differences between the two pictures of this batter?

HINT. It doesn't count that he's facing in different directions—that's what a switch hitter does!

Say What?

Yogi Berra was known as being quite a talker behind the plate. He hoped his chatter would distract the batter! The story goes that in the 1958 World Series, with the legendary Hank Aaron hitting, Yogi kept telling Aaron to "hit with the label up on the bat." Finally, Aaron couldn't stand it any more. He turned to Yogi and said "_____!"

To find out what Hank Aaron said to Yogi Berra, figure out where to put each of the cut apart pieces of the grid.

C'mon Hank, hit it with the label up. Up, up, up, with the label up. C'mon Hank, hit it with the label up...

FUN FACT

Who Says Baseball Is a Slow Game?

World Series games in the first decade of the 1900s usually took about an hour and a half. That's amazing, considering that even regular season games today take close to three hours to play.

Stealing Bases

These teams are some of the first baseball teams in this country! Some are still around, while some have moved to different cities and changed their names. See if you can finish the teams' names by adding the missing letters **B-A-S-E-S.**

Why do hitters like night baseball?

Connect the dots to find the answer to the above riddle.

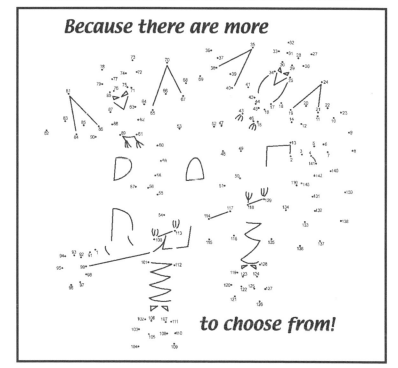

Because there are more

to choose from!

__LTIMOR_ ORIOL__

_O_TON R_D _OX

N_W YORK M_T_

_ROOKLYN DODG_R_

LO_ _NG_LE_ _NG_L_

_TL_NT_ _R_VE_

EVERYTHING KIDS

ANSWERS

Switch Hitter

Why do hitters . . .

Because there are more

to choose from!

Stealing Bases

B̲ALTIMOR̲E ORIOL̲E̲S

B̲OS̲TON R̲E̲D S̲OX

N̲E̲W YORK M̲E̲T̲S

B̲ROOKLYN DOD̲G̲E̲R̲S

LO̲S̲ A̲NG̲E̲L̲E̲S̲ A̲NG̲E̲L̲S̲

A̲TLA̲NT̲A̲ B̲RA̲V̲E̲S̲

Say What?

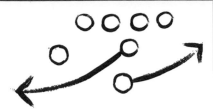

Woofball

Use a light-colored marker to highlight all the letters that are not W, F, or B. Read the highlighted letters to find the silly answer to the riddle!

What do you get when you cross a dog with a football player?

F	A	B	B	F	W
B	W	F	G	W	F
O	F	F	B	F	W
W	B	L	W	B	D
F	E	F	W	N	W
B	F	W	F	F	B
F	B	R	W	F	E
C	W	F	W	F	F
W	E	B	F	I	B
F	B	W	V	F	W
W	E	B	W	B	R

Football GREAT

Glenn Scobey "Pop" Warner

Pop Warner was a standout football player at Cornell University who went on to coach college football for forty-five years, starting in 1895. He is the one who had the idea for players to wear numbers, and he also introduced the huddle and many other common football techniques. He supported a youth football league in Philadelphia in the 1930s. The league eventually became the Pop Warner Conference.

WORDS to KNOW

PLAY: In football, once someone is tackled, the game stops for everyone to line up and start again. A play is the action that happens after the ball is hiked and before someone is tackled. Plays are usually passing plays or running plays.

SACK: When the defense tackles the quarterback before he has a chance to pass the ball, that's called a sack.

OFFENSE AND DEFENSE: The team that controls the ball is the offense. They try to run or pass the ball down the field toward the end zone. The team without the ball is the defense. They try to tackle the player with the ball and knock down or intercept passes.

Way to Play

Use the key to decode the football player's answer to the reporter's question!

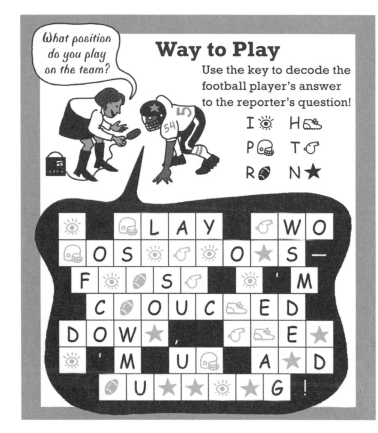

Find the Flag

Can you find the seven times the word FLAG is hidden in this game of flag football?

FUN FACT

The Defense Can Score Too
Sometimes the offense can't move forward because the defense tackles the ball carrier behind the spot where they started the play. If the defense pushes the offense so far back that the ball carrier is tackled in the end zone, the defense gets two points. This play is called a safety.

ANSWERS

Woofball

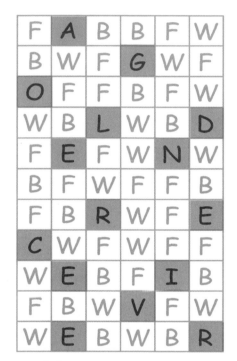

F	A	B	B	F	W
B	W	F	G	W	F
O	F	F	B	F	W
W	B	L	W	B	D
F	E	F	W	N	W
B	F	W	F	F	B
F	B	R	W	F	E
C	W	F	W	F	F
W	E	B	F	I	B
F	B	W	V	F	W
W	E	B	W	B	R

A GOLDEN RECEIVER!

Way to Play

I		P	L	A	Y		T	W	O
P	O	S	I	T	I	O	N	S	—
F	I	R	S	T		I	'	M	
C	R	O	U	C	H	E	D		
D	O	W	N	,		T	H	E	N
I	'	M		U	P		A	N	D
R	U	N	N	I	N	G	!		

Find the Flag

MIDFIELD MADNESS

Let's Play

In each of the soccer balls is the scrambled name of something you need to play soccer—minus one letter! Add the missing letter to complete the word. Then arrange the missing letters to spell one more important piece of soccer equipment.

1.
2.
3.

4.
5.
6.

1. _____
2. _____
3. _____
4. _____
5. _____
6. _____

BONUS: _____

What You Should Put On Before You Get Dressed to Run

Color in all the following kinds of letters:
- last letter of READY
- first letter of SET
- both letters of GO

Then read the uncolored letters to get the answer to the crazy riddle!

```
YOSRGUGYO
NYOSGYSOG
SGDYOOEYG
SSGOYSGOY
OROYSWGYE
OSYAGORYO
```

Spelling Ball

How many words can you find in this soccer ball grid? You may start at any letter, then move from one space to the next touching space in any direction, spelling out a word as you go. You may double back and use a letter more than once in a word (you can spell "eve"), but you may not use the same letter twice in a row (you can't spell "sleep").

The 10-letter BONUS word completes this phrase: Playing soccer is much more fun than watching _____!

SCORE: 10 words = Starter
20 words = Pro **30 words** = World Cup

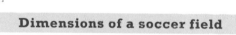
Dimensions of a soccer field

EVERYTHING KIDS'

ANSWERS

Let's Play

1. CLOCK
2. FIELD
3. REFEREE
4. BALL
5. TEAM
6. WHISTLE

BONUS: CLEATS

What You Should Put . . .

RUN-DERWEAR!

Spelling Ball

ALIVE	PAL(S)	SILVER
EVIL	PALE	SLAP
LAP	PALER	SLIVER
LEAP	PERT	TOIL
LION	PET	TOILE
LIVE	REAL	TON
LIVER	REAP	VELVET
NOISE	REAPER	VETO
NOT	RELIVE	VISION
NOTE	REVOTE	VOTE
OVER	SEAL	VOTER

10-letter bonus word: TELEVISION

Play Ball

A baseball player must be sure to follow the rules of the game, or he could get sent to the dugout! You must carefully follow the directions below to learn the word that finishes the following popular saying: "Some people say that playing baseball is as American as eating _____."

1. Print the word BASEBALL. BASEBALL

2. Switch the position of the first two letters.

3. Move the 5th letter between the 2nd and 3rd letters.

4. Switch the positions of the 4th and 8th letters.

5. Change the 6th letter to P.

6. Change the last letter to E.

7. Change both Bs to Ps.

8. Change the 7th letter to I.

Hink Pinks

The answer to Hink Pinks are two rhyming words. Both words of the answer should have the same number of syllables. See if you can score four!

1. The heavier of two batters.

   F _ _ _ _ _   B _ _ _ _ _

2. Where you throw a bad referee.

   U _ _   D _ _ _

3. Nine baseball players shouting at once.

   T _ _ _   S _ _ _ _ _

4. The last part of a baseball game when one team has more points.

   W _ _ _ _ _ _   I _

Who's Who?

Some baseball nicknames are easy to guess. For example, almost all players who have had the last name "Rhodes" have gotten the nickname "Dusty." See how many of the famous nicknames on the left you can match with the real names on the right. Put the number of the correct nickname on the line in front of each real name.

1. The Big Train
2. Tom Terrific
3. Cyclone
4. Joltin' Joe
5. Double X
6. Mr. October
7. The Mick
8. Say Hey Kid
9. Stan The Man
10. Charlie Hustle
11. Wizard of Oz
12. The Big Unit
13. The Rocket

___ Cy Young
___ Jimmie Foxx
___ Joe DiMaggio
___ Mickey Mantle
___ Ozzie Smith
___ Pete Rose
___ Randy Johnson
___ Reggie Jackson
___ Roger Clemens
___ Stan Musial
___ Tom Seaver
___ Walter Johnson
___ Willie Mays

Look! It's "Bubbles" MacCoy!

FUN FACT

The Windiest Ballpark

Candlestick Park—the stadium where the 49ers football team still plays—was built in an unsheltered area right next to San Francisco Bay. Candlestick was known for being very windy and cold, even in the summer. Take a look at highlights of Giants games there and you'll see hot dog wrappers blowing all over the place and fans huddling under blankets. Once the wind blew a pitcher off the mound!

Famous Fungo!

Can you match the silly answers to the funny riddles?

1. What do you call a baseball player who only hits flap jacks?

2. What do you call a baseball player who throws dairy products?

3. What do you call a dog that stands behind home plate?

___ A milk pitcher!

___ A catcher's mutt!

___ A pancake batter!

A "fungo" is actually a ball hit to the infield during fielding practice. Fungoes are hit with a special thin, light bat called a "fungo stick"!

ANSWERS

Play Ball

1. Print the word BASEBALL.   BASEBALL

2. Switch the position of the first two letters.   ABSEBALL

3. Move the 5th letter between the 2nd and 3rd letters.   ABBSEBALL

4. Switch the positions of the 4th and 8th letters.   ABBLEALS

5. Change the 6th letter to P.   ABBLEPLS

6. Change the last letter to E.   ABBLEPLE

7. Change both Bs to Ps.   APPLEPLE

8. Change the 7th letter to I.   APPLEPIE

Hink Pinks

1. The heavier of two batters.

   FATTER BATTER

2. Where you throw a bad referee.

   UMP DUMP

3. Nine baseball players shouting at once.

   TEAM SCREAM

4. The last part of a baseball game when one team has more points.

   WINNING INNING

Who's Who?

1. The Big Train   _3_ Cy Young
2. Tom Terrific   _5_ Jimmie Foxx
3. Cyclone   _4_ Joe DiMaggio
4. Joltin' Joe   _7_ Mickey Mantle
5. Double X   _11_ Ozzie Smith
6. Mr. October   _10_ Pete Rose
7. The Mick   _12_ Randy Johnson
8. Say Hey Kid   _6_ Reggie Jackson
9. Stan The Man   _13_ Roger Clemens
10. Charlie Hustle   _9_ Stan Musial
11. Wizard of Oz   _2_ Tom Seaver
12. The Big Unit   _1_ Walter Johnson
13. The Rocket   _8_ Willie Mays

Famous Fungo!

_2_ A milk pitcher!

_3_ A catcher's mutt!

_1_ A pancake batter!

SUPER SLUGGER

How do you get to the Baseball Hall of Fame?

To find the answer, follow the correct path from PLAY BALL to GAME OVER. Collect the letters along the way, and write them in order on the lines below.

PLAY BALL!

GAME OVER!

_ _ _ _ _ _ _ _ _ _ _ _ _! _ _ _ _ _ _!

WORDS to KNOW

GREEN MONSTER: Famous Fenway Park is one of the majors' two ancient ballparks. To make the field fit inside the available space, the left field fence is very, very shallow—about 305 feet. So, to prevent a gazillion home runs to left field, the fence there is 37 feet high. Because the wall is so huge, and because it's painted green, it's called the "Green Monster."

The "Whole World" Series

While the World Series is played here in America, baseball is popular all over the world! See if you can match the country names with their location to fill in the grid. We left you the W-O-R-L-D S-E-R-I-E-S to help.

TOGO	MEXICO
PERU	ITALY
EGYPT	TAIWAN
IRAN	CANADA
COOK ISLANDS	
PUERTO RICO	
RUSSIA	

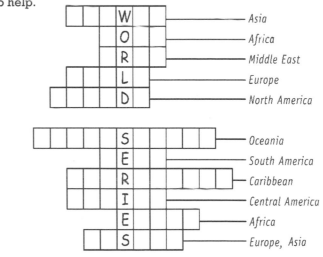

— Asia
— Africa
— Middle East
— Europe
— North America

— Oceania
— South America
— Caribbean
— Central America
— Africa
— Europe, Asia

Baseball Diamond

Can you find six common baseball terms hidden in the diamond grid? Start at a letter and move one space at a time in any direction to a touching letter. You may not use the same letter twice in a word, but you can cross over your own path.

HINT: One of the terms is an abbreviation!

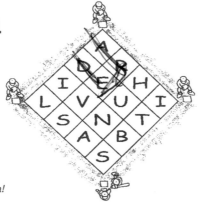

FUN FACT

Best of Seven

The World Series is played as a best-of-seven series: This means that the first team to win four games wins the series, and there can't be more than seven games. In 1903, and again in 1918 through 1920, the series was played as best-of-nine, but it was changed back to today's best-of-seven format.

EVERYTHING KIDS

ANSWERS

How do you get ...

PRACTICE, PRACTICE, PRACTICE!

The "Whole World Series"

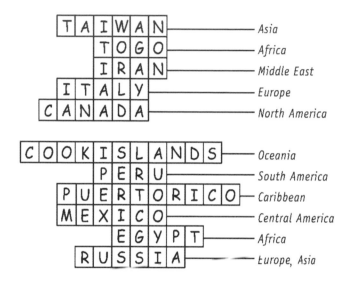

T	A	I	W	A	N					— Asia
	T	O	G	O						— Africa
	I	R	A	N						— Middle East
I	T	A	L	Y						— Europe
C	A	N	A	D	A					— North America

C	O	O	K	I	S	L	A	N	D	S	— Oceania
	P	E	R	U						— South America
P	U	E	R	T	O	R	I	C	O	— Caribbean
M	E	X	I	C	O					— Central America
	E	G	Y	P	T					— Africa
R	U	S	S	I	A					— Europe, Asia

Baseball Diamond

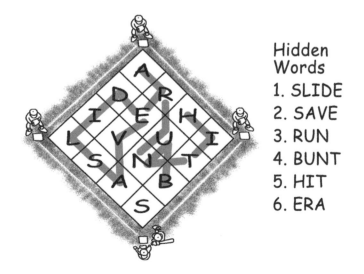

Hidden Words

1. SLIDE
2. SAVE
3. RUN
4. BUNT
5. HIT
6. ERA

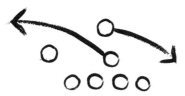

QUARTERBACK SNEAK

P	D	H	O	T	L	H	L	Y	T	E	B	P	I
I	E	O	G	H	K	O	P	J	O	W	R	E	K
U	Q	T	H	O	U	T	G	K	H	A	E	W	J
Y	A	H	J	T	I	H	M	L	O	Q	B	Q	L
R	S	O	K	H	T	T	H	A	T	O	H	A	P
E	Z	G	L	K	Y	P	D	S	J	M	P	S	Y
W	X	H	H	O	P	T	E	H	K	H	O	X	B
Q	C	A	O	J	R	O	Y	O	L	O	D	Z	N
A	V	C	T	K	E	H	H	T	P	T	H	D	M
S	B	V	H	A	W	T	K	T	V	O	P	F	Z
D	N	F	T	S	S	O	L	O	C	H	O	C	A
E	M	E	G	W	D	K	M	F	X	D	G	V	S
H	O	N	H	H	H	J	H	G	Z	T	R	O	H
O	U	J	T	M	O	W	O	H	A	T	E	H	R
T	H	K	O	H	T	S	T	L	O	O	W	T	T
T	K	M	O	J	H	D	T	P	G	H	S	J	O
H	M	L	H	P	O	R	O	R	N	O	F	O	H
K	L	R	F	R	K	F	Y	E	M	A	R	G	D
O	P	Y	H	O	L	O	H	S	H	H	O	F	H
H	J	P	T	J	Y	H	D	W	J	O	M	D	O
O	K	W	O	T	R	T	O	A	S	T	N	E	T
T	I	E	H	L	E	T	G	Z	W	O	B	R	Y
H	T	Q	O	H	D	O	L	X	Y	O	X	Q	O

Wacky Weather

Use a dark marker to color in all the shapes with the letters H-O-T. When you are finished, you will have the silly answer to the riddle.

WHY DID THE STADIUM GET HOT AFTER THE GAME?

Loads of Laundry

There are 48 jerseys to wash and repair before the next game. Figure out how many jerseys each of the five equipment managers is responsible for.

Jonas gets 13 jerseys.

Tom gets twice as many jerseys as Jean.

Jean gets as many jerseys as Lonny.

Lida gets 10 fewer jerseys than Jonas.

Jean gets 5 jerseys more than Lida.

Jonas
Tom
Jean
Lonny
Lida

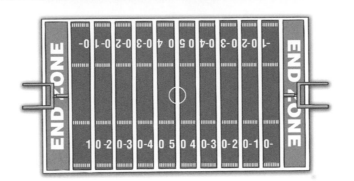

Backfield Buzz

Put the football vocab words in the grid in alphabetical order from top to bottom. When you are finished, read down the shaded column to get the silly answer to the riddle!

Which insect has the hardest time playing football?

OUT OF BOUNDS

HALFBACK

LATERAL

CARRY

DEFENSE

REFEREE

PENALTY

HOLDING

FOUL

GAME BALL

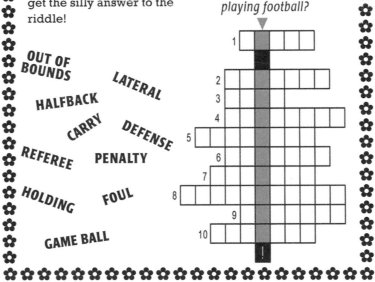

1
2
3
4
5
6
7
8
9
10

FUN FACT

The Importance of Special Teams
Ohio State coach Jim Tressel tells his team that the punt is the most important play in football. Think of how much yardage is traded in just a single punt—nearly half the field! Think about how big a deal it is for a team to block a punt or to return one for a touchdown. That can change a game.

EVERYTHING KIDS

ANSWERS

Wacky Weather

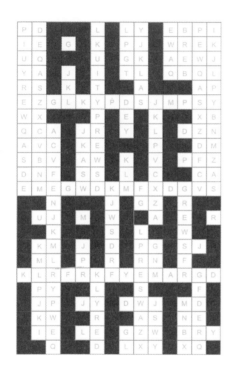

Loads of Laundry

Jonas	13
Tom	16
Jean	8
Lonny	8
Lida	3

Backfield Buzz

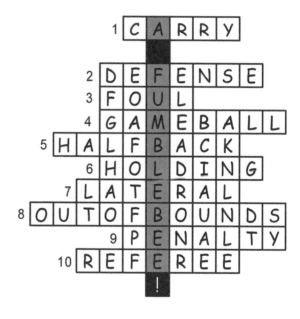

1. CARRY
2. DEFENSE
3. FOUL
4. GAMEBALL
5. HALFBACK
6. HOLDING
7. LATERAL
8. OUTOFBOUNDS
9. PENALTY
10. REFEREE

CORNER KICK CHALLENGE

Go Team!

These fans want everyone to know how much they love the game! Follow the directions below to find out their mighty message.

1. Fill in all the blocks on the left side of signs 1, 2, 3, 6, 7, 9, 11, 12, 15, 21
2. Fill in all the top squares on signs 2, 3, 5, 6, 9, 11, 15, 16, 21
3. Fill in all the bottom squares of signs 1, 2, 3, 9, 11, 12, 16
4. Fill in all the right squares of signs 1, 6, 11, 12
5. Fill in all the squares down the middle of signs 5 and 8
6. Fill in the very middle square of signs 1, 6, 7, 16, 21
7. Fill in the square just below the middle square of sign 1
8. Copy sign 9 onto sign 18 and 19
9. Copy sign 5 onto sign 13
10. Copy sign 7 onto sign 10
11. Copy sign 2 onto sign 4 and 20
12. Copy sign 11 onto sign 17 and 14

Catch!

Get together with a friend and pass the ball back and forth. It's like playing catch, but with a soccer ball! Start by using two touches: you'll "catch" the ball first and then pass it. Once you feel comfortable with that, you can graduate to one-touch passing. See how many times the ball can go back and forth accurately.

Body Building

Answer these questions with words that are also names of body parts.

1. Twelve inches
2. They hold up a chair
3. Two units of corn
4. Hiding place for treasure
5. A baby cow
6. A tropical tree
7. Part of a comb
8. There are two on a clock
9. Needles have threads in them
10. A unit of lettuce

"I think I'll pass this ball with my 'unit of lettuce'!"

Speed Drill

This tiny number puzzle shows a popular kind of defense. What is it?

1
one

Warm Up

These two players know that it's important to warm up before a game. Player "L" is going to run slowly around the field, touching all the light colored dots. Player "D" is going to touch all the dark dots on the field. Follow their paths from number to number with your pencil and you will see a winning soccer move!

EVERYTHING KIDS®

ANSWERS

Go Team!

WE GET A KICK OUT OF SOCCER

Warm Up

Body Building

1.	Twelve inches	foot
2.	They hold up a chair	legs
3.	Two units of corn	ears
4.	Hiding place for treasure	chest
5.	A baby cow	calf
6.	A tropical tree	palm
7.	Part of a comb	tooth
8.	There are two on a clock	hands
9.	Needles have threads in them	eyes
10.	A unit of lettuce	head

Speed Drill

Answer: one on one

EXTRA INNING

The Magic Number

Near the end of the baseball season teams start to figure out the "magic number." This is how many games the leading team must win, and how many games any other team must lose, for the leader to win the pennant (championship in their league).

There's some tricky math here. Pretend you have two teams—Team A and Team X. Team A is the leading team in the league, having won the most games so far. Team X is any other team in the league.

Follow the steps here using the scores from our sample teams. You can use the same steps with your favorite teams!

The season has 162 scheduled games.			
	won	lost	games played so far: 152
TEAM A	93	59	
TEAM X	89	63	

Games TEAM X has won _____

ADD games TEAM X has left _____

SUBTRACT games TEAM A has won _____

ADD the number 1 _____

THE MAGIC NUMBER

> This game goes on, and on, and on...

Extra Innings

Use the clue under the blank space to come up with a word. Write this word in the box. When you add the word "IN", the new word has a totally *different meaning*!

1. _____ IN = to start
   (to plead for money)

2. _____ IN = small house in the woods
   (taxi)

3. _____ IN = springtime bird with red breast
   (steal)

4. _____ IN = heavy, shiny fabric
   (past tense of sit)

5. _____ IN = penguin-like bird with colorful beak
   (short breath out)

What kind of baseball players practice in the Arctic Circle?

Color in each box with a dot in the upper right-hand corner to find the silly answer to this riddle:

> I wonder if they pitch snowballs?

Collectible Cards

Sometimes the most valuable cards are those that accidentally get printed with a few mistakes or differences. Can you find the nine differences between these two cards?

HANK AARON
14
RIGHTFEILDER
⚾ ATLANTA BRAVES ⚾

HANK AARON
44
RIGHTFIELDER
⚾ ATLANTA BRAVES ⚾

Collectible Words

See if you can collect nine words hiding in the word COLLECTIBLE.

Extra Fun: Try to have all nine words use only four letters.

FUN FACT

Dropped Third Strikes

When first base is open or when there are two outs, the catcher must hold on to the third strike. If he drops the ball, he must get the out by tagging the batter or throwing to first base. Usually, the catcher does this without trouble. However, if the third strike was a wild pitch, or if the catcher makes a bad throw to first, the runner could be safe; but the pitcher still gets statistical credit for a strikeout. If this happens, on your scorecard you would write K-E2 (if the catcher made a bad throw) or K-WP (if the pitcher made a wild pitch).

EVERYTHING KIDS

ANSWERS

The Magic Number

The season has 162 scheduled games.				

	won	lost	games played so far:
TEAM A	93	59	
TEAM X	89	63	152

Games TEAM X has won	89
ADD games TEAM X has left	+ 10
SUBTRACT games TEAM A has won	- 93
ADD the number 1	+ 1
THE MAGIC NUMBER	= 7

Extra Innings

1. **BEG** IN = to start
   (to plead for money)

2. **CAB** IN = small house in the woods
   (taxi)

3. **ROB** IN = springtime bird with red breast
   (steal)

4. **SAT** IN = heavy, shiny fabric
   (past tense of sit)

5. **PUFF** IN = penguin-like bird with colorful beak
   (short breath out)

Collectible Cards

Arctic Circle?

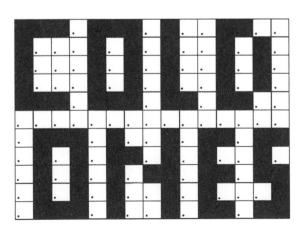

KICKOFF CHALLENGE

Check That Padding!

In most places in the world, the game we call soccer is called football. To avoid confusion, the rest of the world calls our game American football. Who is this soccer player talking to?

What can you catch but not throw? Your breath!

BUT THIS IS A FOOTBALL!

Because of the injuries in football, players wear a lot of padding. Two other less violent versions were invented. Do you know what they're called?

All Mixed Up

It can be confusing to be a fan of fantasy football. Fill in the blanks to see one reason why! There are three possible letters you can use in each blank. Be careful—we've given you one extra fantasy letter!

A H U W

Im_gine t__t
_ f_nt_sy
o_ner __s pl_yers
from t_o
different te_ms.
__en bot_ "re_l"
te_ms pl_y e_ch
ot_er, t_e
f_nt_sy o_ner
_ill _ope t__t
bot_ te_ms
score _ lot!

Which one of these **does not** belong? Helmet, goalie, touchdown, quarterback.

Goalie—the rest relate to football.

Fancy Footwork

Break the letter and number equations to find the silly answer to the riddle.

Why did the official kick Cinderella out of the game?

| A+4 |
| I−1 |
| P+3 |

| X+1 | G−2 |
| B−1 | F+2 |
| V−2 |

| I−4 |
| R+1 | T+3 |
| V−1 | D−3 |

J+3	J+2
L+3	N−2
D−3	D−3

A+2	M+1
G−2	E−4	S−1
G−5	P+2	D+2	A+1

ANSWERS

Check That Padding!

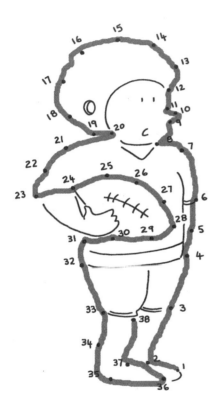

Flag football and touch football are two less violent versions of full-contact football.

All Mixed Up

A H ~~U~~ W

Imagine that a fantasy owner has players from two different teams. When both "real" teams play each other, the fantasy owner will hope that both teams score a lot!

Fancy Footwork

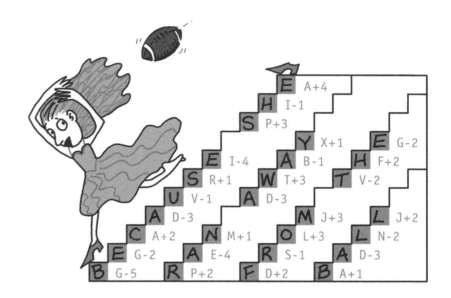

			E A+4	
			I-1	
		S P+3		
		Y X+1	E G-2	
	E I-4	A B-1	H F+2	
	R+1	W T+3	V-2	
U V-1	A D-3			
A D-3	N	M J+3	L J+2	
C A+2	N M+1	O L+3	L N-2	
E G-2	A E-4	R S-1	A D-3	
B G-5	R P+2	F D+2	B A+1	